The Civil War on the Atlantic Coast
1861–1865

by
R. Scott Moore

Center of Military History
United States Army
Washington, D.C., 2015

Introduction

Although over one hundred fifty years have passed since the start of the American Civil War, that titanic conflict continues to matter. The forces unleashed by that war were immensely destructive because of the significant issues involved: the existence of the Union, the end of slavery, and the very future of the nation. The war remains our most contentious, and our bloodiest, with over six hundred thousand killed in the course of the four-year struggle.

Most civil wars do not spring up overnight, and the American Civil War was no exception. The seeds of the conflict were sown in the earliest days of the republic's founding, primarily over the existence of slavery and the slave trade. Although no conflict can begin without the conscious decisions of those engaged in the debates at that moment, in the end, there was simply no way to paper over the division of the country into two camps: one that was dominated by slavery and the other that sought first to limit its spread and then to abolish it. Our nation was indeed "half slave and half free," and that could not stand.

Regardless of the factors tearing the nation asunder, the soldiers on each side of the struggle went to war for personal reasons: looking for adventure, being caught up in the passions and emotions of their peers, believing in the Union, favoring states' rights, or even justifying the simple schoolyard dynamic of being convinced that they were "worth" three of the soldiers on the other side. Nor can we overlook the factor that some went to war to prove their manhood. This has been, and continues to be, a key dynamic in understanding combat and the profession of arms. Soldiers join for many reasons but often stay in the fight because of their comrades and because they do not want to seem like cowards. Sometimes issues of national impact shrink to nothing in the intensely personal world of cannon shell and minié ball.

Whatever the reasons, the struggle was long and costly and only culminated with the conquest of the rebellious Confederacy, the preservation of the Union, and the end of slavery. These campaign pamphlets on the American Civil War, prepared in commemoration of our national sacrifices, seek to remember that war and honor those in the United States Army who died to preserve the Union and free the slaves as well as to tell the story of those American soldiers who fought for the Confederacy despite the inherently flawed nature of their cause. The Civil War was our greatest struggle and continues to deserve our deep study and contemplation.

RICHARD W. STEWART, PH.D.
Chief of Military History

THE CIVIL WAR ON THE ATLANTIC COAST 1861–1865

The Civil War on the Atlantic coast began in comic-opera fashion. While much of the South rejoiced over South Carolina's secession and cursed yet-to-be inaugurated President Abraham Lincoln, fervent North Carolinians seized two Federal forts on the Cape Fear River. Reacting to rumors of Federal ships headed for the North Carolina coast, a newly formed Wilmington militia company, dubbed the Cape Fear Minute Men, set out to capture the dilapidated forts, each garrisoned by a caretaker sergeant. Early in the morning of 9 January 1861, the enthusiastic if ill-equipped militiamen pounded on the outer doors of Fort Johnston, a collection of decayed U.S. Army buildings situated near Smithville, on the entrance channel of the Cape Fear River. The startled Army sergeant quickly surrendered the fort to the invaders, but not before demanding and receiving a receipt to ensure proper accountability of government property. The next day, the Minute Men, flushed with victory, continued downriver to secure the much more imposing, if crumbling, Fort Caswell at the mouth of the Cape Fear, another post held by a lone ordnance sergeant who duly signed it over. The victory proved short-lived. Although likely to secede soon, North Carolina still remained in the Union, and thus the militiamen had unlawfully seized the forts. North Carolina Governor John W. Ellis, maintaining strict legalities, ordered the intruders to find the ordnance sergeants, give them back the forts, and go home. The Cape Fear Minute Men relinquished their conquests and returned to Wilmington, devoid of the glory they imagined should be theirs. The restored caretakers reported the forts none the worse for their ordeal, a dubious qualification given their state of disrepair.

The exploits of the Wilmington militiamen soon faded as the nation rushed toward civil war and newly seceding states seized Federal property and installations. Local forces occupied Fort Pulaski, Georgia, covering the seaward approaches to Savannah, Georgia, and Fort Clinch near Fernandina in northeast Florida. Fort Sumter, blocking the harbor in Charleston, South Carolina, surrendered in mid-April after two days of bombardment. Returning to Forts Caswell and Johnston, North Carolina troops, this time with the governor's approval, took permanent control, as did others at Fort Macon, near Beaufort, a hundred miles up the coast. Although showing the effects of years of parsimonious budgets, the forts soon anchored Confederate defenses on the Atlantic. Around them for the next four years would swirl a succession of naval and land actions, most now forgotten and many unnoticed even at the time. The coastal region from the Outer Banks of North Carolina to the St. Johns River in Florida saw pitched battles, innumerable skirmishes, sieges, raids and retribution, amphibious landings, riverine operations, military occupation, and partisan warfare involving thousands of troops from both sides as well as a major portion of the U.S. Navy. Not insignificantly, the operations also served as the battlefield proving ground for African Americans. If lacking the historical drama of the campaigns in Virginia or the West, those on the Atlantic coast were key elements in a war that slowly strangled the Confederacy.

Strategic Setting

In the years before the Civil War, the ports and waterways of North Carolina, South Carolina, Georgia, and eastern Florida fed the economies of the Atlantic region and, to a large extent, much of the southeastern United States. The primarily agrarian coastal states relied on exports, notably cotton, rice, and naval stores, for their well-being. Cotton flowed through the ports of Savannah, Charleston, and Wilmington to mills in New England

and, equally important, Great Britain. In return, buyers sent the money, manufactured goods, and finished products that sustained the Southern agrarian way of life. Thousands of merchant vessels cleared the harbors, the busiest being Charleston, a center of prosperity and, by mid-century, political agitation. Lesser harbors, such as Jacksonville, Florida, and New Berne, North Carolina, provided local hubs for collection and movement of goods. Linking the ports to each other and to much of the interior stretched a system of tidal rivers, inland sounds, and navigable waterways. In North Carolina, shallow-draft vessels maintained a lively trade on the Albemarle and Pamlico Sounds and the Neuse and Roanoke Rivers. Canals running north from the Albemarle created secure avenues to Norfolk, Virginia; the James River; and the lower Chesapeake Bay. A maze of coastal channels, barrier islands, and sluggish rivers offered protected waterways and outlets to the sea for cotton and rice plantations from northeast Florida into South Carolina.

The introduction of railroads added to the transportation network. A rail line just inland from the coastal islands linked Savannah to Charleston. Branch lines connected the two ports to Columbia, Augusta, and Atlanta, Georgia. The Wilmington and Weldon Railroad coupled Wilmington to Petersburg, Virginia, intersecting at Goldsboro, North Carolina, with a line from New Berne to Raleigh, North Carolina. These waterways and railroads formed an interconnected economic network that sustained the Atlantic states of the South.

Savannah, Charleston, Wilmington, and the numerous rail lines and waterways assumed critical strategic importance with the onset of war. Largely lacking a manufacturing capability, the newly formed Confederacy could not produce military equipage in adequate quantities. For this, it required shipping to move cotton to overseas European markets and to bring back essential cargoes, which in turn depended on the Atlantic ports. The fundamental strategic problem for the new nation centered on thwarting any Federal effort to close the ports, an immediate concern given President Lincoln's declaration of a naval blockade of the South in April 1861. While coastal vessels could use the myriad inlets and waterways to hide and smuggle some goods, they could not compensate for large cargo-carrying blockade runners. Additionally, the ports became key to the South's courtship of foreign support. If kept open, they remained symbols of sovereignty and national viability, essential for diplomatic recognition. Closed to trade by Lincoln, they signified Confederate illegitimacy.

Yet, the traits that made the Atlantic coast so valuable also made it nearly indefensible. With the exception of the captured Federal forts, in 1861 few defenses existed, leaving much of the coastline open to invasion. Moreover, with limited resources and threatened by Federal armies in Virginia and the West, the Confederate government could spare little for coastal protection. Regiments mustering into service departed to other theaters of war, leaving state governors to scrape together what few remaining units, local militia, and armament they could find. The situation quickly exacerbated political cracks in the makeup of the newly declared nation. Built on a foundation of states' rights and highly independent state and local governments, the demands of the central government for troops and resources intensified distrust. To state governors like Joseph E. Brown of Georgia, Francis Pickens of South Carolina, and, later, Zebulon Vance of North Carolina, who could look offshore and see enemy warships, the immediate threat of naval assault trumped anything in far-off Virginia or Tennessee. That Confederate President Jefferson Davis did not share that view only antagonized them. As the war dragged on and the dangers to the coast magnified, friction between the Atlantic coast states and the Davis government grew almost to the breaking point.

Nonetheless, in the summer and fall of 1861, despite shortages in men, weapons, and supplies, the Confederacy took steps to defend its coast. In North Carolina, sand earthworks and pile obstacles blocked Hatteras and other inlets along the Outer Banks while local forces prepared to guard Albemarle and Pamlico Sounds. On the Cape Fear River, a series of fortifications covered the two entrance channels; they would include the most formidable coastal stronghold of the war by late 1864. Charleston harbor and its adjacent inlets and islands boasted numerous batteries. Newly constructed forts on Hilton Head and Phillips Island barred entrance to Port Royal Sound, South Carolina, while other earthworks shielded the coastal railroad from Northern incursions up the inlets and rivers. A maze of obstacles and upstream batteries augmented Fort Pulaski, blocking the seaward entrances to Savannah, while to the south earthworks dotted the St. Johns River. Indeed, nearly every town along the coast seemed to be building defenses to prevent

Federal access and protect blockade runners and smugglers. Lacking a navy, the Confederate government also issued letters of marque. A practice out of fashion with most nations, yet not quite illegal, these letters authorized civilian ships to arm themselves and prey on Northern commerce. Local seafarers took advantage. All along the coast, but especially at Hatteras, North Carolina, and the Outer Banks, privateers began capturing and sinking unarmed merchantmen. If the effects proved to be transitory, the panic caused to shippers was not. Northern merchants demanded naval protection and greatly curtailed their trade with the Caribbean and South America until the Navy could suppress the menace. Despite limited resources, competing priorities, and political friction, the South had managed to create an imposing defensive barrier on the Atlantic coast (*Map 1*).

The Federal government also understood the strategic importance of the seaboard region. A naval blockade, if somewhat precipitously declared by Lincoln shortly after the surrender of Fort Sumter, formed a vital part of Northern war strategy. Desperate to limit the scope of the war to that of a domestic conflict, at least in the eyes of Europe, the blockade served notice to the European powers, especially Britain, that strict neutrality would be enforced. Under international law, it allowed Lincoln to close the rebellious ports, halt outbound trade, and use naval force to prevent any ships, foreign or otherwise, from entering them. Initially, the blockade was more a political gambit than a military reality. Once declared, however, foreign powers were expected to regulate their countries' merchant fleets in accordance with accepted international protocols. Great Britain, a key buyer of Southern cotton and potential supplier of war goods, proved reluctant to challenge those precepts, having exercised them in the past.

The blockade, even if initially enforced only intermittently, struck directly at the Confederate war effort. No amount of smuggling or blockade running could supplant the scale of antebellum trade, especially if foreign nations self-regulated their shipping. It thus formed a crucial part of a grand strategy proposed by Army General in Chief Maj. Gen. Winfield Scott and endorsed by the Navy. Although derided and sarcastically nicknamed the "Anaconda Plan" by the Northern press, General Scott's proposal to cordon off the Confederacy from the sea, while securing the Mississippi River from Illinois to the Gulf of Mexico and then

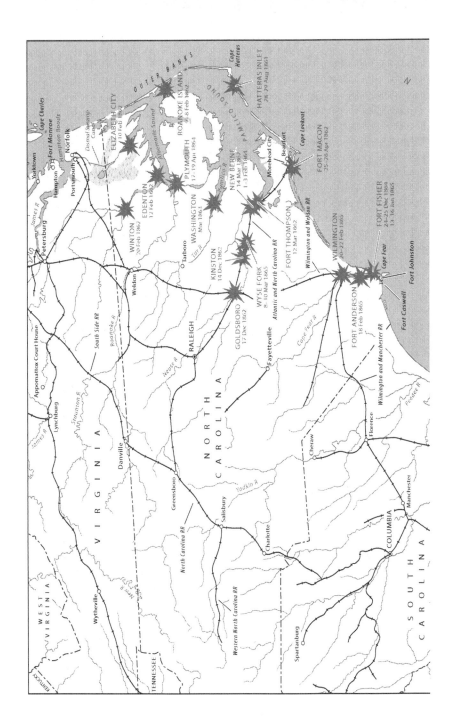

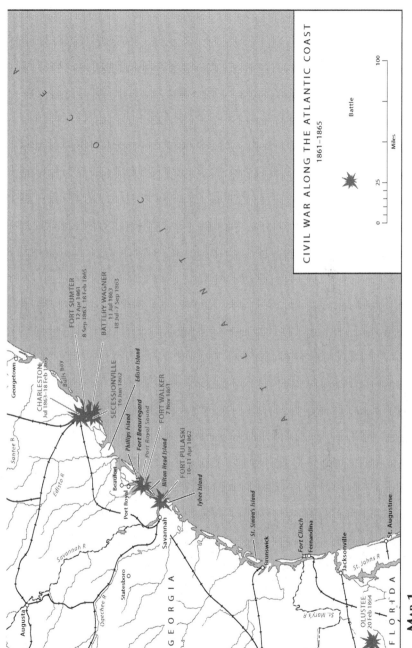

Map 1

defeating the South in pieces, became the strategic basis of the war. The plan required Army-Navy cooperation, not just along the Mississippi, but also along the Atlantic coast. The Navy fully understood the requirements of a blockade at sea, having done so fifteen years before in Mexico, but needed the Army to secure its bases and seize key locations. The Army, although focused on Virginia and the Mississippi, realized it must also play a role in strangling the Confederacy through operations along the coast. Strategically, if not always operationally, the Army and Navy agreed on this basic war aim.

During the summer of 1861, Secretary of the Navy Gideon Welles convened the Commission of Conference, more commonly called the Blockade Board or Strategy Board. Its members consisted of the chairman, Navy Capt. Samuel F. Du Pont, Alexander Bache of the U.S. Coastal Survey, Army Maj. John Barnard, a Corps of Engineers officer with extensive experience along the southern coast, and the board secretary (and active participant) Navy Cdr. Charles Davis. Neither a strategic planning group nor a permanent staff, the commission provided information and recommendations but had no authority for their implementation. Welles directed it to examine the Atlantic coastline and suggest sites for advanced naval bases to support the blockade. The advent of steam-powered ships meant the days of extended duty along remote coasts, with the need for occasional resupply, had ended. Modern ships demanded constant repairs and refitting, as well as regular replenishment of coal, provisions, and ammunition in order to be effective. In 1861, only Hampton Roads, Virginia, and Key West, Florida, remained under Federal control, more than a thousand miles apart and hundreds of miles from blockading stations on the Atlantic coast. Ships sent to watch Savannah, Charleston, or Wilmington could remain on station for just a short period before departing on the long journey back to their bases. Distance dictated that most would spend as much or more time coming and going as on blockade duty. The Navy needed anchorages that could be seized and easily defended. Welles wanted to know the best locations. In addition, he tasked the commission to look closely at the inlets, waterways, and coastal chokepoints that might, if closed, restrict Confederate trade and privateering.

Beginning its deliberations in May 1861, by late summer the commission produced several reports on proposed anchorages, complete with detailed analyses of the geography, hydrography, and defensibility of each site. Turning to operational issues, the commission recommended dividing the single Atlantic Blockading Squadron into two blockading squadrons (the North Atlantic and South Atlantic) separated at the North and South Carolina border. This command structure eased control problems for the Navy but meant Army forces, with no similar division, might find themselves operating across Navy commands. In making these recommendations, the commission assumed Army-Navy joint operations would be for the purpose of establishing bases or cutting off Confederate access to the sea, not harbingers of more extensive inland operations. While that supposition would be stretched somewhat in the coming years, especially in North Carolina, it remained a fundamental tenet for both the Army and the Navy, restricting most coastal operations to seizing and defending advanced bases, sealing off ports, and raiding. The Commission of Conference, in keeping with its charter, did not establish policy or strategy, nor were its recommendations directive in nature. Its reports provided the essential information needed for others to determine where and when coastal operations would be conducted. As the summer of 1861 dragged on and the war saw its first major battles, those decisions were not long in coming.

Operations

THE CAPTURE OF HATTERAS, 1861

While the Commission of Conference continued its work in Washington, the first Atlantic coast operation got under way. Stung by criticism in the press and Congress over the lackluster nature of the emerging blockade (largely unjustified given available resources) and recent depredations by privateers operating off North Carolina, the Navy looked for a chance to make amends. Lincoln pressed for some sort of offensive action. Commodore Silas H. Stringham, commanding the Atlantic Blockading Squadron (not yet divided), received reports that the inlets of the Outer Banks lacked strong defenses and could be easily seized to block exiting privateers. The Army, in the wake of its disastrous defeat at the Battle of First Bull Run, Virginia, also sought a low-risk victory to buttress morale and perhaps dampen Confederate spirits. Maj. Gen. Benjamin F. Butler, commanding

Federal forces at Fort Monroe, Virginia, and recently embarrassed by a defeat at the Battle of Big Bethel, Virginia, developed a plan to do just that and perhaps redeem his reputation. Eyeing Hatteras Inlet, North Carolina, from which privateers emerged almost daily, he sent proposals to Washington outlining a joint expedition to close it. They fell into receptive hands at the War Department and then found their way to Welles, who saw merit in them. The Commission of Conference, although lukewarm to the idea of operations in the sounds of North Carolina, also endorsed the need to close the Outer Banks. General Scott was reluctant to divert the Army's barely trained forces from the defenses of Washington but acceded to mounting pressure and approved Butler's plan. The first Atlantic coastal operation of the war thus began.

A hastily organized Army-Navy force sailed from Hampton Roads on 26 August 1861, fully observed and reported by Confederate lookouts in Norfolk. The fleet consisted of six warships, under the command of Commodore Stringham, in his flagship, the screw frigate USS *Minnesota*, followed by a tug and two troop transports loaded with soldiers. Butler's force consisted of the 20th New York Infantry and three companies of the 9th New York Infantry, better known as "Hawkins' Zouaves" after their flashy French-inspired uniforms and self-promoting commander, Col. Rush C. Hawkins. None of the troops had seen combat, having been mustered into service barely three months earlier. The flotilla arrived off Hatteras Inlet the next day and prepared for battle. Stringham and Butler determined to conduct a two-pronged assault, bombarding the forts from the sea while troops landed unopposed north of enemy earthworks guarding the inlet. If all went well, the operation would be over quickly.

Watching the arrival of the Federal ships, 350 ill-equipped and poorly trained North Carolina troops and their commander, Col. W. F. Martin, had little doubt as to the outcome of the coming engagement. The men manned two hastily constructed earthworks armed with an assortment of cannons and little ammunition. Fort Clark, mounting five guns, faced seaward at the entrance to the inlet. A low-lying earthwork of logs and sand, it stood little chance of seriously challenging the Federal warships. Fort Hatteras, less than a mile away across a marsh bridged by a rudimentary catwalk, covered the sound side of the inlet with an assortment of twenty-five guns. Somewhat better sited, it still lacked both the men and the ordnance to match the force arrayed against it. Most of the Confederate guns had a shorter range than those aboard the Federal ships, which merely had to remain at a safe distance offshore and pound the forts into submission. The Confederate defenders at Hatteras hoped to make a good showing, perhaps inflict some damage on their enemies, and delay the Federal expedition long enough for reinforcements to arrive.

Stringham and his warships began the attack on the morning of the twenty-eighth. Steaming in an oval pattern, the ships opened fire on Fort Clark with broadsides, kicking up huge geysers of sand and quickly silencing its guns. Late in the morning, Butler began landing the 20th New York Infantry two miles to the north, getting the first wave ashore unmolested. The amphibious operation, however, soon went awry. Winds increased, causing boats in follow-on waves to swamp in high surf. Men tumbled into the water, and, after getting only 320 troops to the beach, Butler halted further attempts, leaving the 20th New York alone with few supplies and its waterlogged ammunition largely useless. The beleaguered troops soon received a scare when a Navy gunboat covering the landings opened fire on what appeared to be cavalry bearing down on the exposed beachhead. Panic and confusion among the reported cavalry ensued as horses scattered in all directions, revealing it

Sketch by Alfred R. Waud of Federal troops landing at Hatteras Island, August 1861 (Library of Congress)

to be a terrified herd of local wild ponies. Fortunately for the New Yorkers, the Confederate defenders abandoned Fort Clark after having endured several hours of bombardment. The Federal troops occupied the earthwork, spending a restless night alone and unsupplied, isolated from reinforcements by the winds and surf. Stringham posted two warships offshore to provide gunfire if needed and withdrew the others and the transports to sea to ride out the increasing winds.

The next morning, the winds having subsided, Stringham's warships returned and took station off Fort Hatteras. Out of range of the fort's guns, they bombarded the defenders with impunity and accuracy. The Confederates could do little to prevent the inevitable, even after being reinforced the previous night with troops ferried by steamers from Roanoke. After three hours' punishment, Fort Hatteras surrendered. Butler, despite orders to return his force to Fort Monroe once his troops had neutralized the enemy's earthworks, posted a garrison manned by Colonel Hawkins and his Zouaves. Alarmed by the easy Federal victory and apparent power of naval warships, the Confederates abandoned earthworks guarding Ocracoke and Oregon inlets along the Outer Banks to the north as well. Initially hailed as a great victory by the Northern press, Stringham received criticism from within the Navy for not exploiting it and moving into the sounds. Given the intended purpose of the mission as well as the small size of Butler's force, such criticism was unfair. The success, however, wetted an appetite for coastal operations in both the Navy and War Departments.

THE SOUTH ATLANTIC COAST, 1861–1862

The next operation was not long in coming. At a meeting in September, President Lincoln; Secretary of the Navy Welles; the new Army General in Chief, Maj. Gen. George B. McClellan; and the newly appointed commander of the South Atlantic Blockading Squadron, Admiral Samuel F. Du Pont, met to discuss the need for anchorages to resupply and repair ships engaged in the blockade. Armed with the recommendations of the Commission of Conference, the Navy initially proposed seizing Bulls Bay, South Carolina, and Fernandina, Florida. Although unready for any large-scale land operations, the Army agreed to provide 12,000 troops as a landing force, to be commanded by Brig. Gen. Thomas W. Sherman. Du Pont soon changed the primary objective to Port Royal Sound, South Carolina, which he deemed better suited to the blockading squadron's needs. Port Royal offered perhaps the largest deep-water anchorage on the coast, protected by coastal islands that Union forces could easily defend, and from which they could conduct coastal raids. It was also situated between Savannah and Charleston and was close to the coast of Florida, making the anchorage convenient for his ships. Port Royal had one drawback: the entrance was defended by two Confederate forts, each more formidable than those faced at Hatteras. Nonetheless, Du Pont felt his warships and the troops provided by the Army could dispose of these defenses. By late October, the expedition was ready.

On 29 October, more than fifty warships and transports departed Hampton Roads and headed south. They immediately encountered severe weather that scattered the fleet and threatened to end the operation before it began. When Du Pont's flagship, the USS *Wabash*, reached Port Royal Sound late on 1 November, barely half the ships could be found. Miraculously, in the next few days most straggled in with only minor damage. Unfortunately, at least three transports carrying supplies for the Army, as well as several of the steamers necessary for beach landings, floundered at sea. Worse, the vessel carrying most of the troops' small-arms ammunition did not arrive for several days. Du Pont and Sherman realized a joint naval and land attack would be problematic. Reluctantly, they agreed that the Navy would have to deal with the rebel defenses, with Army troops occupying the islands surrounding Port Royal once the enemy had been neutralized and the passage into the anchorage secured. On 4 November, having sounded the offshore bar and found it passable at high tide, Du Pont moved the ships inshore and anchored within sight of the enemy.

A 2½-mile channel separated two earthworks barring entrance to Port Royal Sound: Fort Walker on Hilton Head Island and Fort Beauregard on Phillips Island. Although each mounted an assortment of guns with only limited supplies of ammunition, their range and size could inflict damage on any ships operating in the restricted waters at the entrance to the sound. A squadron of Confederate gunboats patrolled the inland waters, ready to attack any Federal ships entering the sound. Given the tidal conditions and enemy dispositions, Du Pont decided to engage the forts one at a time at close range from within the sound, using the firepower of his ships to quickly silence the enemy while a small covering force kept the enemy gunboats at bay. On 7 November, he entered the sound and attacked Fort Walker. After three hours, their guns mostly dismounted, the defenders abandoned their earthworks. Shortly thereafter, fearing they might be trapped on the island, the rebels at Fort Beauregard hastily withdrew. Naval landing parties quickly secured the empty forts. Watching from their transports offshore, the troops cheered. Over the next few days, they landed and secured Hilton Head and Phillips Islands. Beaufort, a few miles up the Broad River, fell to Navy gunboats two days later but was not fully occupied until early December. To prevent enemy incursions and to fully secure the anchorage, detachments of soldiers supported by gunboats probed the tidal rivers and islands, as Sherman established his main base on Hilton Head Island.

Officers of the 3d New Hampshire Infantry in camp on Hilton Head Island (Library of Congress)

The loss of Port Royal Sound sent panic through much of coastal South Carolina and Georgia. Plantation owners fled to Savannah and Charleston, many setting fire to their valuable cotton rather than letting it fall into Federal hands. The state governors demanded reinforcements from President Davis. Davis sent them General Robert E. Lee, formerly his military adviser but now appointed to command Confederate forces on the coast. He immediately set about improving the defenses of Savannah and Charleston but worried about how to protect the connecting coastline, realizing he lacked the forces for a strong defense everywhere. Observing a Federal raid up the Coosaw River near Port Royal in December, Lee witnessed the effectiveness of naval guns at keeping at bay any Confederate forces imprudent enough to move within range. Indeed, once landed, the Federal troops, lacking artillery, rarely strayed far from their supporting gunboats. Lee decided that rather than confront the gunboats, he would place his defenses upstream, past the shallow waters preventing gunboats from further ingress. Doing so would leave the island plantations vulnerable but would protect the vital railroad connecting Savannah and Charleston. Stationing forces at key junctions and bridges, Lee established a mobile reserve able to move rapidly along the railroad to challenge any Federal movements inland. By securing the rail line between the two major ports, Lee planned to keep the Federal force at Port Royal at arm's length without tying down large numbers of Confederate troops.

As 1862 began, Du Pont and Sherman looked beyond Port Royal. Du Pont wanted the Army to support the closing of Savannah and to seize such ports as Fernandina and Jacksonville, Florida. After the naval victories at Hatteras and Port Royal, many naval officers convinced themselves that warships could reduce enemy shore defenses without the need of the Army. They saw the Army's role solely as occupying newly won positions. Du Pont became increasingly frustrated at Sherman's unwillingness to provide forces to follow in the wake of the Navy. Yet Sherman had no orders from the War Department to venture elsewhere and was reluctant to scatter his troops along the coast in small garrisons. Additionally, without his shallow-draft launches lost during the transit to Port Royal, Sherman lacked the waterborne transport vessels necessary to support wide-ranging Navy operations. With differing perspectives, missions, and no common commander, Du Pont and Sherman grew increasingly antagonistic toward each other. The situation conspired to limit the effectiveness of the nearly 12,000 bluecoats now posted on the South Carolina coast.

The two commanders finally agreed on two operations: seizing Fernandina and blocking the entrance to Savannah.

Although Du Pont had disregarded the commission's recommendation to secure Bulls Bay by taking Port Royal as his main naval base, Fernandina remained in his plans. Sherman offered a brigade to support its capture. On 2 March, seventeen armed ships and six transports left Port Royal expecting a fight. Unknown to them, Lee had ordered Fernandina abandoned, with the last rebel train leaving the community as the Union ships sailed into view. On 4 March, Federal soldiers landed and occupied Fernandina. The expedition then moved on to seize St. Augustine and Jacksonville, destroying any fortifications it encountered. Gunboats scoured the St. Johns River and its tributaries looking for blockade runners.

In late March, Maj. Gen. David Hunter arrived at Port Royal to assume command of the newly created Department of the South, which encompassed the coasts of South Carolina, Georgia, and Florida. Although Du Pont still wanted to seize as many coastal towns and ports as possible, Hunter concluded he could not garrison them all and thus pulled many of his troops back to Port Royal from Florida. Although he left the garrison at Fernandina, his troops withdrew from Jacksonville without consulting Du Pont, a move that infuriated the admiral and set the tone for later squabbles.

Even as operations continued in northeast Florida, Federal attention turned to Savannah. The Navy, after reconnoitering the water approaches, determined its ships could not bypass Fort Pulaski nor get into position to bombard it without excessive risk. As long as the fort remained in Confederate hands, it threatened Port Royal and sheltered Savannah's blockade runners. Sherman and Du Pont thought a combined naval and land assault on Savannah might be possible, but planning stalled when the two disagreed on details, and reinforcements needed for the operation were unavailable. Instead, the War Department sent orders to reduce Fort Pulaski by siege and dispatched heavy artillery for the purpose. Capt. Quincy A. Gillmore, a Regular Army engineer tasked to plan the siege, chose Tybee Island, about a mile off Fort Pulaski, as the best location for the arriving batteries. As the artillery arrived in February and March, soldiers toiled in the muddy soil to erect new battery sites.

By 10 April, Gillmore had succeeded in positioning eleven batteries of artillery, including mortars, nine large 30-pound Parrott guns and converted James guns, and four naval guns transplanted from Du Pont's ships. When the Fort Pulaski garrison refused to surrender, the massed batteries opened fire. Built in the 1840s to withstand smoothbore cannons, the fort's brick outer works could not long withstand the modern rifled guns on Tybee Island. After just a day, Union fire had reduced the wall facing Tybee Island from a height of more than seven feet to half that, with large cracks in the masonry as well as an ever-widening hole. The next day, the fort surrendered when shells began passing through the wall and exploding dangerously close to the magazine. In just thirty hours, Gillmore had demonstrated the power of modern rifled artillery against fixed fortifications. At little cost, the Federals had closed the port of Savannah.

The damage to Fort Pulaski from the Federal bombardment
(Library of Congress)

By the spring of 1862, the Confederacy no longer controlled its coast south of Charleston. A pattern now emerged that persisted for much of the war. The islands and inlets of South Carolina and Georgia became contested zones in which skirmishes abounded, but pitched battles rarely occurred. Federal troops supported by gunboats raided along the tidal waterways, foraging for food, confiscating cotton and lumber, destroying buildings and goods deemed useful to the enemy, and freeing large numbers of slaves whose owners fled inland. Local Confederate troops patrolled the islands and harassed Federal outposts, but mounted concerted challenges only when Federal expeditions moved up the tidal rivers toward the railroad. Economically damaging and the source of much angst, the almost continuous operations kept the South Atlantic coast in constant turmoil.

The Burnside Expedition, North Carolina, 1862

As Federal forces seized Fernandina and prepared to lay siege to Fort Pulaski, another expedition readied itself to invade the sounds of North Carolina. Disappointed with the failure to exploit the capture of Hatteras, both services looked to control the inland waterways and perhaps threaten Norfolk and Richmond, Virginia, from the south. In the fall of 1861, Brig. Gen. Ambrose E. Burnside organized and equipped a division capable of conducting operations in coastal waters. He intended to move into the sounds of North Carolina and penetrate the state via its waterways. With War Department approval, he recruited regiments from New England and New York composed of men whose civilian occupations as fisherman and coastal mariners made them familiar with waterborne operations. In addition, he acquired gunboats, transports, and surfboats to support, move, and land his soldiers. Although finding it difficult to procure transports, largely because the Navy bought most of the available ships for the expanding blockade, Burnside nonetheless mustered nearly 15,000 troops and a leaky assortment of barges, transports, gunboats, tugs, steamers, and surfboats in Annapolis, Maryland, by January 1862.

General Burnside
(Library of Congress)

The Navy agreed to support the expedition, providing warships and shallow-draft gunboats under the command of Flag Officer Louis M. Goldsborough, newly appointed commander of the North Atlantic Blockading Squadron. On 9 January, Burnside's force departed Annapolis for Hampton Roads to join Goldsborough's fleet. Two days later, the joint expedition sailed south for Roanoke Island, its first objective.

Blocking the only passage between Albemarle and Pamlico Sounds, Roanoke Island held the key to the inland waterways.

Possession of the island would enable the Federals to control much of eastern North Carolina. General McClellan, contemplating his campaign up the Virginia Peninsula to capture Richmond, saw Burnside's effort as a useful supporting operation, perhaps able to draw off Confederate forces or even forming a pincer from the south as his main army moved directly on Richmond from the east. Despite the strategic value of Roanoke, the Confederate government could spare few resources to defend it. In all, barely 2,000 newly raised troops from North Carolina and Virginia occupied the island and surrounding waters. Three forts defended the island and the passage, all indifferently equipped with obsolescent or poorly maintained pieces and manned by inadequately trained soldiers. The forts on Roanoke Island faced toward the water in expectation of a naval attempt to force the passage. A Federal attack up the island from the south seemed improbable due to its swampy terrain. Beyond some pickets, the southern half of the island lacked defenses, with only a battery of artillery and some supporting infantry blocking the single road and causeway in the center of it. The Confederate Navy deployed a varied collection of gunboats, nicknamed the "mosquito fleet," in the passage itself, mostly coastal steamers with a cannon mounted forward. On the mainland side, a canal barge—anchored in the mud and mounting a battery of field pieces—completed the defenses.

Arriving off Hatteras, shaken by severe weather and forced to wait several more days until heavy seas subsided, the Federal armada soon discovered that the inlet's depth of six feet prevented many of the larger warships and Army transports from crossing into the sound. By grounding a ship and then using the fast-moving tides to dig out the sand around it, thus creating a deeper channel, the fleet finally crossed on 4 February. Further delays occurred as the ships repaired damage caused by the weather. Goldsborough and Burnside, on good terms, used the time for detailed planning and coordination. Finally under way, the expedition arrived off the southern end of Roanoke on the morning of 7 February. Goldsborough moved quickly to engage the mosquito fleet and neutralize the enemy forts. He soon silenced their guns and chased away the gunboats, suffering little damage to his own ships. In midafternoon, Burnside began landing at Ashby Harbor to the south, while Goldsborough's ships and Army gunboats lobbed shells into the surrounding forest. Some gunboats were partially manned by detachments of the 99th New York Infantry, self-styled the "Coast Guard" and trained as shipboard gunners and landing parties. In a notable innovation, the troops landed from flat-bottom boats boarded by climbing down ladders placed on the sides of the transports and then towed to the beach by steamers. Just offshore, the steamers turned sharply, releasing the tow ropes and slinging the landing boats toward

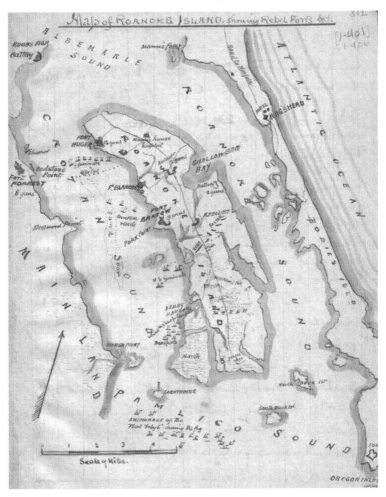

Sketch map of Roanoke Island made shortly after the battle
(Library of Congress)

the shoreline. Oarsmen then took over and brought them to the beach. By midnight, three brigades landed virtually unopposed and prepared to move north in the morning.

Despite the state of Confederate defenses and the successes of the previous day, Burnside's troops faced a daunting task. Just one road ran north through the island, with deep swamps on either side. A mile from the landing area, the island narrowed, and the terrain greatly favored the defender. Mud and quicksand-filled swamps virtually cut the island in two, crossed only by a causeway. Here the Confederates placed a battery of three guns, supported by infantry. They worried little about their swamp-infested flanks, which they deemed impassable. Burnside felt otherwise. Ordering one of his three brigades to attack straight up the road, he directed the others to move through the bogs and brush to his right and left. Early on 8 February, the attack began. Led by the 25th Massachusetts Infantry, the center brigade charged. Enemy artillery and rifle fire stopped the regiment, inflicting severe casualties. The 10th Connecticut Infantry passed through the Bay Staters from behind, advanced a little farther but suffered a similar fate. On the flanks, largely unnoticed by the defenders, the other brigades moved forward. The swamps proved to be passable, and, although slowed by muck and brambles, the Federals soon enveloped the Confederate line. Seeing mud-encrusted blue-clad soldiers emerge on their right and left, the defenders broke and fled. On the main road, the 9th New York Infantry, having spent the previous months tediously guarding the forts at Hatteras, charged through the stalled Connecticut troops and overran the remaining defenders. With the Confederates in retreat, Burnside moved his force forward, mopping up stragglers and forcing the surrender of the forts, all three of which could offer little resistance to the Federal troops in their rear. Although suffering less than a hundred killed or wounded in battle, virtually the entire Confederate force on Roanoke Island surrendered.

The Federals quickly exploited their victory. Goldsborough dispatched a squadron of gunboats to Elizabeth City, North Carolina, to deal with the remnants of the mosquito fleet, destroying it and capturing the town on 10 February. Two days later, Edenton fell to a naval landing party that burned a schooner and spiked some antiquated cannons before departing. On 20 February, Hawkins and his regiment burned Winton on the Chowan River after receiving sporadic gunfire from local militia. Although later claiming departing Confederates set fire to the town, his actions brought him the lasting enmity of North Carolina and suspicion from his own commanders. Nonetheless, Burnside placed Hawkins in command of a brigade at Roanoke and ordered him to keep Albemarle Sound subdued. Gunboats with detachments of soldiers aboard soon roamed the sound, seeking out Confederate forces, confiscating supplies, seizing vessels, and closing down coastal trade. With his rear secure, Burnside turned southward toward New Berne and the Neuse River.

The defeat at Roanoke shocked the Confederate government and created panic in much of eastern North Carolina. The Federals seemed capable of depositing troops anywhere their gunboats could take them. The governor insisted that his state troops stay in North Carolina rather than go north to Virginia, a demand largely unheeded by the Confederate government. Yet Confederate leaders, both in North Carolina and in Richmond, realized New Berne likely would be the next target. With a railroad line leading to the state capital and connecting the port to the Wilmington and Weldon Railroad at Goldsboro, New Berne provided an important terminus for food and supplies gathered from the surrounding countryside. In Confederate hands, the city offered a base to attack Federal gains at Roanoke and Hatteras and to counter any moves against the port of Beaufort. Under Federal control, New Berne would threaten all of eastern North Carolina and could serve as a base for a larger invasion of the state or a move on Wilmington to the south.

With McClellan's massive army readying itself for a spring offensive in Virginia, the Confederate government could spare few troops to defend North Carolina. Nonetheless, the state managed to retain a few regiments, if only partially trained and inadequately equipped. To prevent Federal ships from sailing up the Neuse River, several forts guarded the water approaches to New Berne, but the rebels did little to defend against a landward attack along the road and rail line leading west from Morehead City. Confederate Brig. Gen. Lawrence O. Branch established a defensive line about six miles from the city, with the Neuse River on his left and swampy pine forest on the right. With only about 4,500 raw troops, the short line anchored on Fort Thompson on the Neuse River offered the best terrain to stop an advancing Federal army. Branch positioned most of his forces between the river fort and the railroad that split the center of his line. He placed the remaining men to the right with their flank resting on the forested swamp. A brickworks next to the railroad divided the two sets of breastworks, causing the right to draw back about 150 yards and create a small gap between the two wings of his force. Branch compensated by posting a militia battalion near the works and a reserve regiment nearby. As word reached him of a Federal expedition marshaling at Hatteras, Branch hastened to finish the defenses and prepare his troops.

On 11 March, Burnside embarked nearly 11,000 troops aboard transports at Roanoke, sailing to rendezvous with warships anchored at Hatteras. Although Goldsborough departed to deal with the emergency brought on by the Confederate ironclad CSS *Virginia* at Hampton Roads, his subordinate, Cdr. S. C. Rowan, assumed command in his place. Rowan and Burnside worked well together. Sailing up the Neuse River, Burnside landed unopposed near Slocum's Creek on 13 March. His three brigades then marched on New Berne, seventeen miles distant, while gunboats moved parallel along the river, occasionally firing just ahead of the advancing troops to ward off any unseen enemy. By nightfall, despite drenching rains that turned the approach into a nightmare of mud, the three brigades closed on the Confederate defenses. Burnside planned to attack the next morning, with two brigades abreast and one in reserve. Much like the enemy he faced, the railroad split his forces and divided the attack into two semi-independent efforts. To compensate, he centered his reserve brigade to the rear, prepared to reinforce either wing. Naval gunboats stood in the river, ready to provide fire support and to suppress Fort Thompson.

The assault immediately broke down, as the right brigade attacked before the left could get into position, and stalled in the face of four North Carolina regiments crouched behind parapets. Multiple charges on the Confederate earthworks failed to gain ground. The 10th Connecticut Infantry then moved to within 200 yards of the enemy and delivered covering fires for their charging comrades while Rowan's gunboats bombarded the defenders. Some naval shells landed among the Federals, creating confusion and a few friendly casualties. Rowan, noting the damage done to the rebel works by his heavy 9-inch guns, later stated unapologetically, "I thought it better to kill a Union man or two than to lose the effect of my moral suasion." The 10th Connecticut's rifle fire and Rowan's naval guns notwithstanding, the attack on the right failed.

Meanwhile, Burnside's left brigade began its attack. The leading regiment, the 21st Massachusetts Infantry, spotted the gap in the center of the Confederate lines and moved to

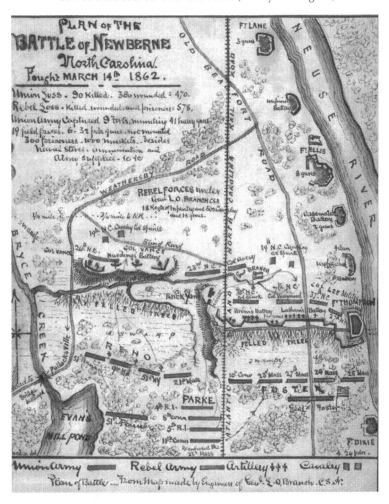

Sketch map of the Battle of New Berne compiled from Federal and Confederate sources after the battle (Library of Congress)

exploit it. Scattering the North Carolina militia battalion, the Massachusetts soldiers broke through then faced right, flanking the enemy breastworks from behind. A melee erupted as the surprised Confederates tried to plug the hole in their lines and the Federals sought to widen it. Elements of the 21st Massachusetts soon found themselves nearly surrounded, but they refused to budge. The tide eventually turned when the Union reserve advanced into the gap and routed the remaining defenders. A staunch Confederate stand quickly transformed into a disorderly rout. Many of Branch's troops did not stop until they reached New Berne nearly six miles away, burning the Trent River bridge behind them to delay Burnside's pursuit. Rowan's gunboats, however, moved up the Neuse River and arrived at the city wharf late on 13 March, just as the last Confederates set fire to stores and buildings and retreated up the rail line westward toward Kinston. The next day, U.S. troops ferried across the river and entered the city, adding to the damage by going on a looting spree that Burnside ended with difficulty.

After establishing defenses to forestall any Confederate counterattack, Burnside directed Brig. Gen. John G. Parke to seize Morehead City and Beaufort, thirty miles to the east on the coast, and then force the surrender of the Confederate garrison at Fort Macon. This would eliminate Confederate forces in his rear and open a supply line from the port at Beaufort to New Berne, using the railroad that connected the two, while capturing the harbor at Beaufort for the North Atlantic Blockading Squadron. Parke moved rapidly, entering Morehead City on 22 March and Beaufort the next night. Startled citizens awoke to find their town occupied by blue-uniformed soldiers. Other than burning bridges in the Federal path, the few Confederates in the area offered little resistance. Nor could they. Southern authorities had shifted most of the troops originally posted near Morehead City to defend New Berne, leaving behind scarcely 400 men at Fort Macon and a few local militia and cavalry in the countryside. Reconnoitering a landing site on Bogue Banks out of range of the guns of the fort, Parke shuttled across troops and artillery, intending to lay siege to the post. Inching his lines forward to within a mile, he hid his cannon and mortar batteries behind sand dunes until ready to open fire, posting pickets to deflect any enemy attempt to disrupt his preparations. On 23 April, Parke sent a surrender ultimatum to the fort commander, who promptly rejected it despite his nearly hopeless situation. Two days later, the Federal bombardment began, augmented by offshore Navy warships. Parke's guns and mortars soon found the range, in no small part due to an Army signal officer in Beaufort with a clear view of the fort. He spotted the fall of the shells and sent corrections using flags. Unable to mount an effective response and with the fort's masonry walls cracking, the defenders of Fort Macon formally surrendered on 26 April.

OPERATIONS IN EASTERN NORTH CAROLINA, 1862–1864

With the capture of New Berne and Fort Macon, Burnside next moved to consolidate his hold on the rest of eastern North Carolina. His forces occupied Washington and Plymouth and carried out a series of raids and marches intended to keep the enemy off-balance. Meanwhile, gunboats patrolled the sounds and rivers, sometimes landing troops to destroy Southern works or commandeer supplies. Even before Fort Macon fell, a Union force under the command of Brig. Gen. Jesse Reno had landed at Elizabeth City, ordered by Burnside to destroy the locks on the Dismal Swamp Canal connecting Norfolk with Albemarle Sound. Burnside feared that the CSS *Virginia* might venture south through the canal. The Confederate ironclad had recently attacked the Federal fleet at Hampton Roads and dueled with the USS *Monitor*. It now threatened the canals to the south from its base at Norfolk. Reno's force ran into Georgia troops sent to protect the locks, and, after a day's battle, the Federal expedition withdrew before it could accomplish its mission. Fortunately, the rebels scuttled and burned the *Virginia* on 11 May when Norfolk became untenable, due to the advance of General McClellan's army up the Virginia Peninsula toward Richmond. In addition, they disabled the locks, fearing Federal gunboats might use the canal to attack Norfolk.

Around New Berne and southward, Union patrols clashed with Confederate troops, burned saltworks, and foraged for food. Then, in late June, the War Department directed Burnside to reinforce McClellan's army on the Virginia Peninsula. The general obliged, departing New Berne for Virginia with 7,000 men while leaving Brig. Gen. John G. Foster to command the remaining forces in North Carolina. For the next several months, Foster's troops, too weak for offensive action, strengthened defenses around their enclaves and patrolled the countryside, occasionally carrying out small foraging expeditions. In September and October, Confederate troops deployed from Virginia tested the Federal garrisons at Plymouth and Washington, penetrating the towns before withdrawing under fire from gunboats. Foster reacted by dispatching relief columns, but the raids caused little beyond local alarms.

Not until late fall had Foster enough forces to move west toward the Wilmington and Weldon Railroad. The reinforcements came in the form of New England militia pledged to nine months of Federal service. Foster had the new men defend New Berne, freeing his long-term veteran regiments for expeditions inland. In November, Foster launched a raid toward Tarboro. After a few skirmishes along the way, he learned of a large enemy concentration converging on Tarboro and turned back. The next month, he marched to interdict the Wilmington and Weldon Railroad where it crossed the Neuse River at Goldsboro. On 11 December, a column composed of infantry, artillery, and cavalry left New Berne, its movement timed as a diversion for the Army of the Potomac's operations at Fredericksburg, Virginia. Three days later, at the Neuse River near Kinston, Foster clashed with troops from North and South Carolina, inexplicably positioned with the river to their backs. When the Federals flanked the Confederate line, an orderly retreat by the South Carolinians became a rout after rebels set the bridge across the Neuse on fire before the retreating troops could cross it. Only with great difficulty did the Confederates re-form, but not before Foster captured nearly 400 rebels trapped on the wrong side of the river. The Federal column continued toward Goldsboro, skirmishing with enemy forces that paralleled its advance from the other side of the Neuse. On 17 December, it arrived at the railroad bridge just a few miles from Goldsboro, guarded by three North Carolina regiments, which soon withdrew under Union cannon fire. Foster's troops burned the bridge, cutting the Wilmington and Weldon Railroad, although not for long. Confederate engineers soon repaired the damage. Far from his base and facing enemy troops hastily dispatched from Lee's army in Virginia after the Battle of Fredericksburg, Foster withdrew to New Berne.

For the next two years, a war of patrols, raids, small battles, and foraging expeditions devastated eastern North Carolina. Federal troops continually emerged from New Berne, Washington, and Plymouth, or appeared from gunboats patrolling the sounds to challenge local Confederate forces, replenish food, and assert their control. Locally recruited Unionist irregulars roamed west and north from bastions resupplied by their Northern sponsors. Their depredations spread fear and destruction, although perhaps no more than that inflicted by Confederate partisans also operating in the area. A buffer zone emerged that defied control by either side. Federal commanders, repeatedly called on to dispatch regiments to Virginia or South Carolina, rarely mustered sufficient strength to do more than defend their enclaves and harass the enemy. In the winter months, Confederate soldiers sent from Virginia to find supplies added to the misery of a region already suffering from Federal foraging.

Occasionally, Lee sent a division from the Army of Northern Virginia to strike at the Federal defenses, more to placate the North Carolina governor and populace than to achieve any real military gains. In March 1863, he sent Maj. Gen. Daniel H. Hill to attack New Berne. Failing to make headway, Hill shifted his forces to Washington to besiege the town but was unable to capture it before Federal gunboats broke through with timely reinforcements and supplies. In January 1864, Lee sent Maj. Gen. George E. Pickett to assault New Berne from three sides, supported by Confederate gunboats based on the Neuse River. The Confederates launched a series of attacks during the first three days of February against the Federal brigade holding the town. The defensive works around the city proved formidable, and coordination of the attacks was poor. Pickett suffered much the same fate as Hill the year before and soon returned to Virginia.

Lee replaced Pickett with Brig. Gen. Robert F. Hoke, a native North Carolinian. Hoke concentrated on the isolated Federal garrison at Plymouth, on the Roanoke River, just west of Albemarle Sound. He struck on 17 April 1864 with two brigades and artillery, supported by the CSS *Albemarle*, an ironclad built on the Roanoke River and nearly impervious to the smaller Federal gunboats near Plymouth. Abandoning their outer breastworks, the Federals withdrew to the town's inner defenses. Early on 19 April, the *Albemarle* appeared, sailing past the river defenses and sinking or dispersing the gunboats in its path. Hoke then launched his final attack, overrunning the Federal lines. Disorganized, with the enemy in the streets, and cut off from evacuation or support from the river, the garrison surrendered. A few days later, the Federals evacuated Washington. Unable to challenge the enemy ironclad, the U.S. Navy momentarily ceded control of Albemarle Sound, but the Confederates failed to exploit their advantage. Lee demanded troops from the Carolinas to forestall the campaign of Union Army General in Chief Lt. Gen. Ulysses S. Grant in Virginia, stripping away much of Hoke's force.

During a spirited engagement with U.S. Navy gunboats in May, the *Albemarle*, its machinery poorly maintained, received enough damage to force it to anchor up the Roanoke River for repairs. The ironclad still posed a threat even if unable to venture forth for the moment. In October 1864, U.S. Navy Lt. William Cushing crashed a tug over the ironclad's protective boom and drove a spar torpedo under the ironclad, sinking it at its moorings. The rebels soon evacuated Plymouth and Washington, followed closely by Federal troops who reoccupied the towns.

CHARLESTON AND THE BATTLE OF SECESSIONVILLE, 1862

While the war ebbed and flowed in North Carolina, the focus of Federal operations on the coast shifted to Charleston, South Carolina. The emotional lure of the city seemed to hypnotize the Lincoln administration. Assistant Secretary of the Navy Gustavus V. Fox railed at Charleston, calling it "Satan's Kingdom," and repeatedly demanded that the South Atlantic Blockading Squadron attack the city. To Fox, Charleston and Fort Sumter personified treason. As early as November 1861, following the seizure of Port Royal, the Navy had pressed the War Department to send troops to help take Charleston. The Army estimated that any effort to capture Charleston would require thousands of men who it would have to divert from other more important theaters of operations, and it denied the Navy's request. To the War Department, so long as the port could be blockaded, such a distraction seemed unnecessary. Nearly 12,000 soldiers already served along the South Carolina and Florida coasts; no more could be spared.

By the summer of 1862, however, the Army could no longer avoid pressure to attack Charleston. General Hunter had assumed command of the newly created Department of the South in March 1862, and he immediately took a more aggressive stance than had his predecessor. In April, he sent forces to occupy

General Hunter
(Library of Congress)

Edisto Island, South Carolina, eastward toward Charleston, moving closer to Charleston's outer defenses. On 12 May, Robert Smalls, a slave pilot aboard the Charleston steamer *Planter*, commandeered the vessel while the captain and officers were ashore. Sailing it past the harbor defenses, he surrendered to an offshore Navy blockader. Smalls brought news that Confederate forces had evacuated Coles and Battery Islands, opening the entrance to the Stono River and a potential back door to Charleston via James Island, which lay immediately southwest of and abutting Charleston. General Hunter and Admiral Du Point acted quickly, agreeing on a plan to attack Charleston's defenses from the rear by way of James Island. With the southern approaches to the island and the Stono River clear of enemy forces, the way looked open to the city while bypassing the many batteries that protected the entrance to the harbor.

Hunter loaded one division aboard transports, sailed them up the Stono River, and landed them on James Island on 2 June. He marched another division across Johns Island to be ferried over to James Island. Navy gunboats covered the attack with the fall of their shot spotted and adjusted by Army officers signaling from shore to ship, an innovation previously tested during raids on the tidal rivers near Port Royal. Naval shells dropped in front of the troops, clearing woods of Confederate skirmishers, at times firing beyond the direct observation of the gunboats. The Federals greatly outnumbered their enemy, but Hunter was convinced otherwise. Fearing a Confederate counterattack, he had his men dig in. For more than a week, they skirmished with local Confederate forces but did not move. Hunter then departed for Port Royal, presumably to gather reinforcements, leaving

Brig. Gen. Henry W. Benham with strict instructions not to attack until ordered.

While the Federals dallied, the Confederate commander in Charleston, Maj. Gen. John C. Pemberton, rushed troops to James Island. At a chokepoint between two tidal creeks about a half mile from the village of Secessionville, they built Fort Lamar, a *W*-shaped earthwork manned by more than 700 infantry and artillerymen. The fort barred any move to cross James Island. Using other regiments of infantry positioned at various points on the island, Pemberton created a reserve ready to respond to any Federal move (*Map 2*).

Aware of the enemy measures, Benham grew impatient. Having received no instructions from Hunter, he decided to strike on 16 June. An assault force totaling nearly 3,500 men attacked in the early morning, hoping to surprise and overwhelm Fort Lamar. A second force covered the Federal left, advancing in parallel on the other side of a small tidal creek. As the main force moved on Fort Lamar, the 8th Michigan Infantry came within 200 yards of the enemy before grapeshot and rifle fire tore into it. On its right, the 79th New York Infantry scaled the fort's parapet and fought hand to hand with the rebel defenders before the Southerners forced it back. Repulsed, the Federals regrouped and launched two more attacks, with little success. A quarter mile to the left, across the tidal creek, the 3d New Hampshire Infantry attempted to flank the fort but could not wade through the tidal mud separating it from the enemy. Firing from across the creek, the regiment nonetheless swept the facing parapets of defenders. Success proved short-lived. Confederate reinforcements rushed to the battlefield and cannon fire from the fort soon struck the New Hampshire regiment. The best chance had been lost. About midmorning, the attack ended when Benham ordered his troops to withdraw, having suffered nearly 700 casualties. Outraged on hearing of the failed assault and seeking to deflect criticism, Hunter relieved Benham for disobeying his orders, then evacuated James Island.

If Hunter possessed a lackluster combat record, he achieved lasting notoriety for his actions with regard to freed slaves. A staunch abolitionist, upon assuming command at Port Royal in 1862, he had issued an order emancipating slaves in the department. Lincoln was not yet ready to take such a measure, in part because he feared alienating the slave-holding border states that

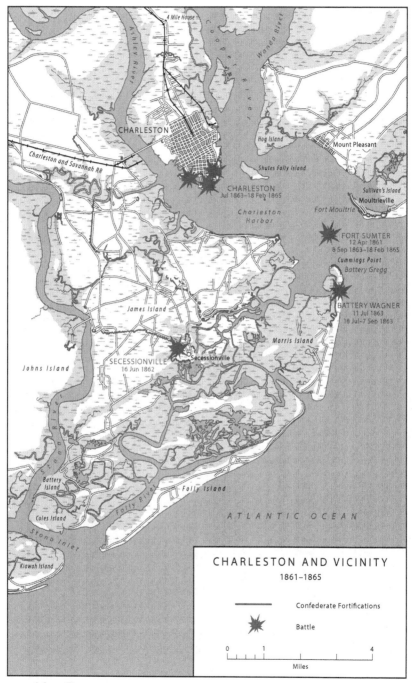

MAP 2

The 1st South Carolina Infantry (African Descent) on parade, Beaufort, South Carolina, 1863 (Library of Congress)

remained loyal to the Union, and he quickly revoked the order, but Hunter was undeterred. Already managing a large population of former slaves, which he paid to grow crops on the sea-island plantations in the Port Royal area as well as to perform labor for the Army, the general launched raids explicitly to free slaves. He forcibly removed slaves from the islands or armed them to prevent the return of white slave owners or local militia. Going a step further, Hunter raised a regiment of former slaves, the 1st South Carolina Infantry (African Descent) in the summer of 1862. Although initially employed as labor troops and soon disbanded by the War Department, the seeds had been planted. Indeed, one company, posted to distant St. Simon's Island in Georgia to ward off Confederate marauders, could not be reached and remained on duty. In November, the company, under instructions from Brig. Gen. Rufus B. Saxton, military superintendent of plantations in the area, raided nearby islands, burning saltworks, confiscating foodstuffs, and removing slaves. Despite Lincoln's previous directive, by the end of the month and with Saxton's active complicity, the 1st South Carolina comprised more than 500 men, soon to be commanded by Col. Thomas W. Higginson, a New England abolitionist and former supporter of abolitionist John Brown. Higginson continued to build his regiment, even sending recruiting parties as far south as Fernandina.

In late 1862, the president caught up with his field commander and issued an Emancipation Proclamation that expressed the government's intent to free all slaves living in rebel territory. On 1 January 1863, the 1st South Carolina Infantry formally received a set of regimental colors and a month later mustered into Federal service. It was one of the first African American regiments (predating the more famous 54th Massachusetts Infantry by several months) and its soldiers were almost exclusively former slaves from the coastal region. The 2d South Carolina Infantry formed in May 1863, with two more units to follow later in the summer. In early 1864, all were reflagged as United States Colored Troops infantry regiments. These regiments paved the way for the thousands of African Americans who fought in the Civil War, a large number of whom would serve along the Atlantic coast.

Morris Island and Battery Wagner, 1863

Army interest in Charleston waned for more than a year but not so for the Navy. Secretary of the Navy Welles continually sought ways to build the image of the Navy, much of which remained unseen to the public in a thankless blockade. He distrusted joint Army-Navy operations, grousing that the Army claimed the glory for successes and blamed the Navy for failures, a charge that had some grounds after Hunter claimed the Navy had failed to support his troops at Secessionville. In April 1863, Secretary Welles ordered Du Pont, against the admiral's advice, to mass his ironclad monitors and run past Fort Sumter and the batteries of Charleston. Welles believed, based on past experiences early in the war, that ships' guns could overcome any fortification and this seemed like an opportunity to prove that theory and achieve a decisive naval victory. The effort failed against the defenses of Charleston Harbor. In an aftermath filled with recriminations, Welles replaced Du Pont with Rear Adm. John A. Dahlgren. The War Department also relieved Hunter, replacing him in June 1863 with Maj. Gen. Quincy A. Gillmore, the man who, as a captain, had engineered the surrender of Fort Pulaski fourteen months earlier.

Gillmore believed a coordinated Army-Navy campaign could take Charleston. Recently arrived reinforcements enabled him to sustain operations from Port Royal to the south and to undertake operations at Charleston. Meeting with Dahlgren on 4 July, Gillmore laid out a plan to march his troops across undefended Folly Island, cross over to Morris Island, and then overrun the two fortifications protecting the mouth of the harbor, Battery Wagner and Battery Gregg. The advance across Morris Island would be supported by ships firing into the flanks of the enemy. With Morris Island taken, heavy guns emplaced on Cummings

Point could neutralize Fort Sumter and cover the Navy as its ships fought past the channel defenses into Charleston, opening the city to capture. Dahlgren readily agreed to the plan.

On 10 July, the operation began. Covered by artillery on Folly Island and Navy monitors firing on Confederate defenders, Gillmore's troops crossed to the southern tip of Morris Island. Overcoming resistance with the aid of naval gunfire, they advanced to within several hundred yards of Battery Wagner by nightfall. Blocking the way forward, Battery Wagner abutted a marsh and brush on one side and the ocean on the other. The only approach consisted of a narrow strip of open sand just wide enough for one regiment at a time. Soldiers from North and South Carolina manned the fortification, which was built of sand, earth, and logs in angled walls protected by an outer ditch. They sheltered in bombproofs against artillery and naval gunfire, able to quickly sortie to parapets if assaulted. Victory for an attacker was only possible by brute force.

Buoyed by the rapid progress up Morris Island and hoping to quickly overwhelm Battery Wagner, Gillmore ordered an attack for the next morning. But he failed to notify the Navy, whose guns had been a key part of the day's success. Unaware of Gillmore's plan, Dahlgren's ships did not support the assault on the Confederate strongpoint. Early in the morning of 11 July, the 7th Connecticut Infantry, followed by the 76th Pennsylvania Infantry and 9th Maine Infantry regiments, advanced to within a few hundred yards of the walls before coming under fire and charging. Some of the Connecticut troops reached the crest of the wall, engaging the defenders at close quarters. They went no farther. Regiments behind the Connecticut soldiers, jammed together by the narrow terrain and subjected to intense fire, broke and fled, leaving the forward troops isolated. The Federals suffered more than 300 casualties in just a few minutes. The attack was a disaster.

Chastised by this setback but undaunted, Gillmore planned a second assault. He positioned artillery and reinforced his forces while offshore ships systematically shelled Battery Wagner with their 11- and 15-inch guns. On 18 July, confident artillery and naval gunfire had much reduced the fort's defenses, Gillmore formed ten regiments of infantry in a column of three brigades. Terrain dictated the formation, a drawback that Gillmore hoped the bombardment and sheer numbers would overcome. Leading the attack was the 54th Massachusetts Infantry, an African

View of Battery Wagner after its capture
(Library of Congress)

American unit made up largely of freedmen from the Northeast, which had only recently arrived in South Carolina and was eager to prove itself.

After a final preparatory bombardment from artillery and naval guns lasting nearly the entire day, Gillmore ordered his troops forward shortly before sunset. Unfortunately, in the growing dark the Navy could no longer observe its shot well enough to avoid endangering the attack, and it ceased its bombardment as the assault began. This left the enemy time to emerge largely unscathed from his hardened shelters to man the ramparts before the Federals could close on the fort. Channeled into a killing zone, the assault dissolved in confusion. The 54th Massachusetts broke through the palisade and started up the fort's sloping wall, only to be greeted by canister and rifle fire that left it shattered. More regiments pushed in behind to meet the same fate. Officers fell, regiments intermingled, some soldiers fled, and order disintegrated. While a few troops managed to breach the ramparts, those not killed or wounded huddled in the ditch before the wall or in shell craters farther out. Elements of the 6th Connecticut Infantry and 48th New York Infantry scaled the seaward wall and entered the fort but went no farther. The second brigade, observing the fate of those to the front, balked when ordered to attack. Nonetheless, when the brigade eventually moved forward and joined those pinned down at the base of the wall, all charged. For a few moments, success seemed possible. But the third brigade, waiting in reserve, inexplicably never advanced. The Confederate defenders sealed off any penetrations and continued to fire into the killing zone. Gillmore sounded retreat. Of more than 5,000 Federal troops engaged, nearly a third had been killed or wounded. The 54th Massachusetts mustered barely 50 percent present for duty the next day.

Repulsed twice, Gillmore decided to besiege the rebels on Morris Island while simultaneously neutralizing Fort Sumter. In a textbook operation, trenches and traverses worked their way toward Battery Wagner. Artillery and naval gunfire kept the Confederates pinned down on Morris Island while slowly reducing Fort Sumter to rubble. Heavy artillery began lobbing shells into Charleston itself, using church spires as aiming points. Although of limited military impact, the bombardment of the city added a dimension to the campaign unseen in earlier operations. Civilians now became targets. By early September, the siege lines reached to within a few hundred yards of the walls of Battery Wagner. The defenders, enduring increasing casualties and faced with an overwhelming enemy both on land and offshore, notified General P. G. T. Beauregard, commanding Confederate forces in Charleston, that they could no longer hold out. As Gillmore prepared for a final assault, they slipped away. On 7 September, Federal troops bloodlessly occupied a nearly destroyed Battery Wagner and moved on to Cummings Point. Morris Island had finally fallen.

CHARLESTON UNDER SIEGE

With the Federals occupying Morris Island, Fort Sumter faced an onslaught. Battered by Federal bombardment by land and sea, the artillery departed on Beauregard's orders. Infantry occupied the fort, more a symbol of defiance than any real threat to the Federal forces. Yet it continued to attract Army and Navy attention. Dahlgren organized a landing force of 500 sailors and marines and prepared to seize Fort Sumter on the night of 8 September. He failed to notify Gillmore, whose artillery overlooked the fort. Compounding the lack of coordination, Gillmore planned a similar operation the same night, unknown to Dahlgren. Only at the last minute did Gillmore learn of the Navy's plans, and in a pique, he directed his commanders not to

Federal troops on Morris Island watch the USS New Ironsides *firing a broadside at the Confederate defenses of Charleston.*
(Library of Congress)

support the Navy. If the Navy assault boats reached Fort Sumter first, then the Army troops were to draw off and offer no help. They did as ordered. The Navy attack proved to be a disaster. Caught in the act of landing but unable to cross the rubble and remaining fort walls, the sailors and marines succumbed to enemy rifle fire from within the fort and artillery fire from across the entrance channel at Fort Moultrie. Those not killed were captured.

Fort Sumter's defiance notwithstanding, with the capture of Morris Island the Union had effectively closed the port of Charleston. U.S. commanders could not justify the potential cost of a full-scale assault on the city, so they chose to remain outside instead, the infantry defending Morris Island and the approaches to the Stono River. Skirmishing became an almost daily affair. Occasional landings on James Island kept up the pressure and tied down Confederate troops. At the harbor entrance from October to December 1863, a sustained Army and Navy bombardment pounded Fort Sumter into a largely useless pile of rubble, but the many other Confederate harbor defenses kept the Navy from sailing up the channel. In early 1864, Federal gunners began a steady bombardment of the city that would continue for much of the next year. Charleston did not fall until 18 February 1865 when isolated and evacuated in the face of Maj. Gen. William T. Sherman's march through South Carolina. Until then, it remained hemmed in and under constant attack, unable to contribute to the war effort and subjected to the punishment many in the North felt it deserved.

The Battle of Olustee, 1864

As the siege of Charleston dragged on, active operations continued elsewhere in the Union Army's Department of the South. A constant stream of expeditions by detachments of soldiers loaded aboard gunboats moved up and down the inlets and rivers from Edisto Island, South Carolina, to the St. Johns River in Florida. Raiding, skirmishing, foraging, defending forward outposts, garrisoning towns and coastal fortifications, and conducting an occasional foray inland occupied the daily lives of soldiers sent to the department. The largest expedition occurred in early 1864 in northeast Florida. Envisioned as a large-scale raid to seize naval stores and prevent supplies and cattle from being shipped from Florida through Georgia, as well as to induce the Unionist factions in the region to swear allegiance, the operation involved nearly 6,000 troops under the command of Brig. Gen. Truman A. Seymour at Port Royal. Embarked on transports escorted by gunboats, the force sailed for Florida in early February 1864. Landing at Jacksonville on 7 February, the troops fanned out to seize key crossroads, railroad bridges, and enemy supplies. The 40th Massachusetts Infantry, mounted on horses and equipped with repeating rifles, penetrated nearly fifty miles inland. Confederate forces, mostly widely scattered local militia, offered little opposition.

Unfortunately, early success succumbed to indecision. Seymour had hesitated for several days after landing, unsure of his next move. The delay allowed the Confederates to dispatch reinforcements, to include veteran Georgia troops rushed from Charleston. Gillmore finally ordered Seymour to consolidate his forces and establish a defensive line anchored on Jacksonville, and he appointed Seymour commander of a newly created District of Florida. Now holding what he considered to be an independent command, Seymour decided after concentrating his forces to advance west to cut the railroad line over the Suwanee River on which cattle and foodstuffs moved north. On 20 February, Seymour's advance guard bumped into cavalry screening Confederate forces assembling near Olustee. What began as a skirmish quickly escalated into battle as both sides fed units forward. A crisis arose when the 7th New Hampshire Infantry, moving up to relieve forward elements, received contradictory commands, lost order, and buckled in the face of advancing enemy troops. On its left the 8th U.S. Colored Troops stood fast but retreated after suffering nearly 300 casualties. Only the timely arrival of a New York brigade prevented a Federal rout. Restricted by pine forests and boggy ground, the antagonists were locked in a bloody struggle, with the Confederates slowly gaining the advantage. A final charge by the Georgians forced back the Federals. Sensing defeat, Seymour ordered a withdrawal, with the 54th Massachusetts and the 35th U.S. Colored Troops acting as rear guard. Thus protected against Confederate pursuit, the Federals retreated to Jacksonville. Despite the defeat at Olustee, Union forces occupied Jacksonville for the remainder of the war, blocking inland access to the sea and conducting raids into the countryside.

Olustee marked the last major battle in the Department of the South. Raids and skirmishing persisted among the sounds, islands, and waterways, while artillery continued to shell the city of Charleston and its outlying forts. Port Royal remained the largest and most important base for the South Atlantic Blockading Squadron, requiring an Army garrison to ensure its security. In the spring of 1864, General in Chief Grant ordered many of the veteran units serving in Florida and South Carolina north to join his campaign against Lee. Regiments that had served in the department during many of its major operations would now fight alongside the Army of the Potomac in the siege of Petersburg. When Sherman's army approached Savannah at the end of its "March to the Sea" in late 1864, the troops garrisoning the coastal islands conducted expeditions up the rivers from Port Royal to divert Confederate troops and threaten the railroad between Charleston and Savannah. In January 1865, part of Sherman's army shifted from Savannah to Beaufort, South Carolina, to begin its march though the Carolinas. Those troops left behind provided security and maintained control of what had become a backwater while the war moved north.

The Wilmington Campaign, 1864–1865

By the fall of 1864, only one major seaport remained open to the Confederacy. On 5 August 1864, Rear Adm. David G. Farragut's ships had fought their way past the defenses of Mobile Bay, Alabama, effectively closing the last major Gulf port. With Charleston under siege, New Berne occupied, and much of the Atlantic coast subject to raids and occupation, Wilmington, North Carolina, now provided the sole access for rebel blockade runners. Upwards of seventy ships operated from the port, smuggling essential goods, war supplies, and not a few luxuries. Lee's army in Virginia depended on them for many of the weapons, supplies, and ammunition otherwise unavailable to an increasingly exhausted South. Yet Wilmington seemed almost impervious to interdiction. The city lay more than twenty-five miles from the mouth of the Cape Fear River and well out of range of naval guns. The entrance to the Cape Fear River and the approaches to the city bristled with forts, earthworks, artillery batteries, and defensive lines. Two inlets, separated by miles of shallow water, islands, and shoals, made blockading problematic. For more than three years, the U.S. Navy had unsuccessfully tried to stop the blockade runners. To do so demanded more than just warships.

The key to closing Wilmington rested with Fort Fisher, a mammoth earthwork located between the sea and the river on a peninsula formally named Federal Point but unofficially renamed Confederate Point by local authorities. Shaped like an inverted *L*, the mammoth fort consisted of a series of elevated battery positions designed to withstand the strongest naval bombardment. Its sea face, nearly a mile long from south to north just above the high-water line, held nearly twenty long-range guns, mostly 8- and 10-inch Columbiads, in protected batteries. The Mound Battery anchored the southern end, rising over forty feet and mounting two heavy cannons. It not only fixed the end of the fort and overlooked the inlet, it provided a beacon for blockade runners. The land face cut for 500 yards across the peninsula from the sea to the Cape Fear River. It mounted twenty-two smaller cannons, in one- and two-gun batteries separated by traverses shielding them from enfilading naval gunfire. A palisade and electronically detonated torpedoes (land mines) were meant to break up any assault before it reached the walls. At the river end, a pair of fieldpieces guarded the only entrance to the fort via a road that crossed a stream immediately to the front of the gate. At the apex of the land and sea faces rose the 32-foot-high Northeast Bastion, a combination firing battery and battle command post that allowed observation over the entire fort and its approaches. Inside the fort, a flat plain contained barracks and three mortars, while sturdy bombproofs dug into the fort's walls protected the garrison and ammunition magazines. The entire fort was constructed of sand and earth covered in sea oats and grass designed to absorb the impact of naval shells. About a mile west and south of the fort, at the tip of Federal Point, stood Battery Buchanan, mounting two 10-inch Columbiads and two 11-inch smoothbores overlooking the inlet and river. In Confederate hands, Fort Fisher kept Wilmington open.

On 2 September 1864, Assistant Secretary of the Navy Fox and General Gillmore, recently reassigned to Washington, D.C., but seeking more active duty, met with Grant at his headquarters at City Point, Virginia, to discuss their plan to seize Fort Fisher. President Lincoln had expressed interest in the plan but was unwilling to order Grant to back the operation if, in the commanding general's opinion, it was unwise to do so. Stalemated by Lee at Petersburg and with Sherman stalled before Atlanta, Grant saw little reason to siphon off troops for a risky campaign he considered of secondary importance and a Navy responsibility. He did, however, understand the political importance of the city. Wilmington remained a symbol of Confederate sovereignty so long as ships could enter and leave. Additionally, the summer battles in Virginia and Georgia had cost too many lives for what much of the population in the North saw as little gain. War weariness threatened to end the conflict short of a Union victory. Lincoln needed some good news from the front with the presidential election just a few months off, and the plan appeared to offer a chance for some. Grant reluctantly agreed to support the expedition, with the caveat that he would do so only when troops became available.

No sooner had Grant tepidly endorsed the plan than the strategic situation changed. On the day Grant met with Fox and Gillmore, Sherman captured Atlanta. He then advised Grant to support the operation against Wilmington as a useful adjunct to his maturing plans to march to Savannah. The appointment of Admiral David Dixon Porter, known and admired by Grant since the Vicksburg Campaign in 1863, to command the North Atlantic Blockading Squadron finally convinced him to support the expedition. Although still not fully committed, in late September he directed 6,500 troops from General Butler's Army of the James to be prepared to sail to Wilmington and appointed Maj. Gen. Godfrey Weitzel to command the force. Grant, however, hedged his bets; while earmarking the troops and directing Weitzel to plan for the expedition, he withheld orders to dispatch it. Delays in gathering the troops and procuring transports further slowed preparations. Grant nearly withdrew Army support when he received reports that the Confederates knew an operation to be forthcoming, but he gave in to continued pressure from Porter and the Navy Department.

In early December, Grant learned that the Confederates were withdrawing troops from Wilmington and Fort Fisher to reinforce those confronting Sherman in Georgia. Sensing an opportunity, he released Weitzel. Much to Admiral Porter's chagrin, however, Grant made no attempt to stop General Butler, nominally Weitzel's commander, from assuming active command of the expedition. Whether deferring to Butler's prerogatives as commander of the Department of Virginia and North Carolina or seizing the chance to remove, even if for a short while, the often inept but politically connected Butler from operations around Petersburg, Grant's inaction produced an immediate effect. Any prior goodwill between the Army and Navy evaporated. Porter thought Butler a fool and still rankled over a feud dating to their service at New Orleans two years before. Butler equally detested Porter. The two rarely met, using messages and subordinates to communicate. Fully aware of Fort Fisher's formidable defenses, Butler distrusted the Navy's ability to neutralize them. Instead, he proposed to load a ship full of explosives, beach it opposite the fort's sea face, and detonate it, blasting a gap in the wall and stunning the garrison into defenselessness. Porter thought the idea impractical but agreed to supply the flat-bottomed USS *Louisiana* for the purpose. Nearly two more weeks elapsed before the Federals could ready the ship, strip it down to look like a blockade runner, and pack it with more than 200 tons of explosives. Finally, on 12 December Porter's armada, the *Louisiana* included, sailed from Hampton Roads, followed two days later by Butler's troop transports.

A comedy of errors and poor coordination ensued. Porter's ships put in to Beaufort, North Carolina, to coal and to complete packing the *Louisiana*. Unaware, the Army transports arrived at the designated rendezvous point off Wilmington on 15 December to find no Navy ships. Three days later, Porter arrived, advising Butler by dispatch boat that the Navy would detonate the explosives-packed ship that night. Surprised and enraged, Butler sent Weitzel to Porter's flagship demanding the detonation be delayed until it could be coordinated with the landing of his troops. Neither Butler nor Porter talked directly, instead using dispatches and subordinates. A storm struck the fleet on

19 December, halting all operations for the next two days. Butler steamed his transports to Beaufort for refueling and provisioning while the storm blew over. He then notified Porter, whose ships remained off Cape Fear, that the Army transports would return on 24 December. Porter chose not to wait. On the night of 23 December, the *Louisiana* proceeded toward the fort, crewed by a few sailors. When about 600 yards offshore, the crew set the charges and abandoned ship. Shortly before 0200 on 24 December, the *Louisiana* exploded, sending flames and water skyward but doing little else. Inside Fort Fisher, the garrison assumed a blockade runner, chased aground by a Federal gunboat, had been set afire and its magazines exploded. When the sun rose in the morning, Porter sent a ship to assess the damage done. It reported Fort Fisher unscathed.

With daylight, Porter's ships commenced firing on Fort Fisher in anticipation of Butler's arrival and a Christmas Day landing. The shelling lasted all day and, from the sea, looked to be effective as geysers of sand flew and smoke covered the fort. Unobserved, however, the garrison sat safely, if uncomfortably, in bombproof shelters while the ramparts above them absorbed the bombardment. In fact, many of the shells overshot the walls and impacted on the plain behind, destroying barracks but doing little else. Butler's transports arrived that night. Fuming over the Navy's actions, he sent Weitzel to meet with Porter and work out a landing plan. On Christmas Day, the attack resumed. Late in the morning, troops went ashore from surfboats and barges north of Fort Fisher, covered by gunboats. The fort remained silent, a sign taken by some, to include Porter, that the bombardment had done its work. By late afternoon, more than 2,500 troops landed, with another 4,000 men waiting offshore in reserve. As the lead brigade turned toward the land face of Fort Fisher, winds began to rise, threatening to halt further landings. The Confederates emerged from their bombproofs to man the fort's guns, most still intact. Faced with the dilemma of only part of his force ashore, rising winds, and a still strongly defended fort, Butler ordered a withdrawal. He then promptly departed for Hampton Roads, even while many of his troops remained stranded on the beach by high winds. Porter was outraged at what he thought was cowardice, incorrectly believing his ships had silenced Fort Fisher. But he could do little more than support the troops still ashore. Two more days elapsed before all could be ferried back to their transports. Porter then took his ships to Beaufort.

The failure at Fort Fisher produced immediate effects. Lincoln recalled Butler, who never held another command. Porter blamed the Army, convinced the fort could have been taken by storm after the Navy had all but neutralized its defenses. The allegations stung the War Department and Grant, who pledged support for another attempt to seize Fort Fisher. The promise also reflected a renewed strategic interest in Wilmington. On the day Butler landed his troops near Fort Fisher, Sherman telegraphed Lincoln offering Savannah as a Christmas present. He proposed to march north through the Carolinas, and, while Grant originally intended to shift Sherman's army to Petersburg, he approved the new plan. Once ambivalent toward Wilmington, Grant now viewed the port as an essential forward base for Sherman's campaign. In early January 1865, he placed Maj. Gen. Alfred H. Terry in command of nearly 9,000 troops for a second assault on Fort Fisher. In written orders, Grant directed Terry to cooperate closely with Porter, warning him that no misunderstandings should come between the two. Terry, a modest and capable veteran who had commanded a brigade during the assaults on Battery Wagner and a corps at Petersburg, impressed Porter when they met at Beaufort on 8 January. They quickly bonded, personally meeting each day for detailed planning.

General Terry
(Library of Congress)

On 12 January, the expedition got under way, led by nearly sixty warships ranging from small gunboats to the USS *New Ironsides* with its fourteen 11-inch Dahlgren guns. Twenty-two transports carried Terry's landing force of three small divisions, to include one from the recently formed XXV Corps composed entirely of African American regiments, along with field artillery, heavy siege guns, and engineers. Facing the Federal force, the Fort Fisher garrison mustered barely 700 men, although Lt. Gen. Braxton Bragg, recently appointed to command the defenses of Wilmington, promised reinforcements to the fort's commander, Col. William Lamb, should an attack occur. In December, in response to Butler's landings, Lee had dispatched 6,000 men under the command of Maj. Gen. Robert F. Hoke to Wilmington from the defenses of Petersburg. Although they had arrived too late to be a factor, they had remained in Wilmington. In the event of another assault on Fort Fisher, Bragg planned to move Hoke's division down Federal Point to block any movement toward Wilmington and threaten the Federal rear. Bragg meant to protect the city, believing Fort Fisher largely capable of defending itself.

Shortly after dawn on 13 January, Porter's fleet positioned itself off Fort Fisher and the beaches to its north while the troops prepared to board boats, many rowed by sailors. Directly covering the landing site, Navy guns opened fire into the woods and brush behind the beaches, intent on keeping any Confederates at bay. Despite high surf that drenched many of the soldiers, the operation went smoothly. Indeed, some troops stopped on the beach to build fires and dry out while bands greeted follow-on waves. After two hours and with several brigades ashore, skirmishers advanced inland (*Map 3*).

Bragg ordered Hoke to take up positions on Federal Point. A brigade deployed by river steamers went ahead, while the remainder marched the fifteen miles from the city. Hoke, convinced he faced a much larger force and leery of the naval guns, chose to dig in and defend against attack rather than to strike at the landing. About 350 South Carolinians, loaded on boats, managed to reach Battery Buchanan and make their way to Fort Fisher, where Lamb could muster barely a thousand defenders to meet Terry. Meanwhile, Porter's main battle line opened fire on the fort, focusing on the gun positions and the land face and its protective palisade. Tacitly admitting the previous bombardment may not have been wholly effective, he gave strict orders to his captains to carefully observe the fall of shot. The naval bombardment systematically whittled away at the defenses. Terry, meanwhile, consolidated his beachhead and late that night the division from the XXV Corps extended a defensive line across the peninsula two miles north of Fort Fisher. They worked all night building breastworks and prepared to stop a

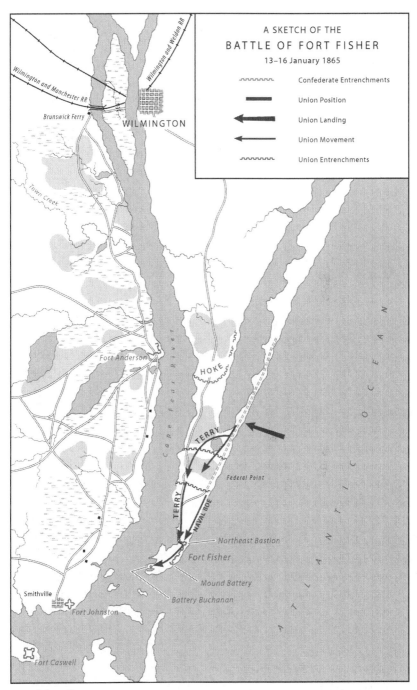

Map 3

still-anticipated counterattack by Hoke's Confederates less than a mile away. Behind the defensive line, the rest of Terry's force readied to move south.

The next day, the remainder of Terry's force landed, along with much of the artillery and some of the siege guns. The African American soldiers continued to strengthen the defensive line while Hoke made little effort to probe it. In midmorning, Porter's ships again closed in and opened fire. They disabled nearly all of the guns along the land face, tore gaps in the protecting palisade, and killed or wounded Confederates attempting to effect repairs or return fire. The two assault divisions moved slowly toward Fort Fisher, erecting a continuous set of rifle pits and remaining concealed in the woods beyond the beaches as they did so. Terry personally crept to within 400 yards of the wall to see the defenses for himself and finalize his attack plan. Observing the damage from the naval bombardment and unsure of the size or intentions of the Confederate force to his north, he determined to attack Fort Fisher the next day rather than to settle into a lengthy siege. Terry then rowed out to Porter's flagship to coordinate the assault.

Terry's plan exploited a weakness he had observed. His main effort would be directed near the river, where the land face ended at the road entrance to the fort. Two enemy fieldpieces protected the gate and a battery on the wall overlooked the open ground to the front. Nonetheless, Terry felt his troops could cross the ground and overwhelm the defenders while avoiding fire from many of the guns farther down the land face. The Federal forces would attack in a column of brigades, each to be committed on Terry's order. Once inside, they would move along the land face, rolling up the batteries one at a time from west to east. The two commanders agreed on a system of flag signals to keep supporting naval gunfire just ahead of the advancing troops, preventing Confederates from reestablishing their defensive positions. Porter then added a twist. He intended to land a naval brigade of more than 2,000 marines and sailors armed with cutlasses and pistols to overwhelm the Northeast Bastion at the other end of the land face. Although surprised by Porter's plan, Terry said little. Grant had strictly enjoined him to cooperate fully with the Navy. So far, cooperation had been excellent. The naval attack would not affect Terry's plan, so he did not object.

During the night, Terry advanced his brigades through the wooded areas near the river. They settled into shallow rifle pits within a few hundred yards of the land face. The 15th New York Engineers built battery positions along the river for heavy artillery to ward off any Confederate attempt to bring reinforcements down the river or to shell the Federals from gunboats. In midmorning on 15 January, the naval brigade landed. Despite their officers' efforts, the sailors, undrilled in land tactics, formed into a loose column. Marines deployed forward as sharpshooters, under orders to pick off any enemy who might poke up his head. By 1500, they stood within 600 yards of the fort, in full view of the Confederates. On the far right, Federal soldiers deployed to their final positions, led by sharpshooters who advanced to within 200 yards of the fort. Arrayed in a column of four brigades, each deployed in line to lessen casualties. At 1530, Terry signaled Porter to shift his bombardment, and, five minutes later, Porter's ships sounded their whistles to start the attack.

Already under sporadic cannon and rifle fire, the naval brigade charged in an elongated mass of shouting sailors and marines, with the officers quickly losing control. When the naval bombardment shifted to the sea face, the unsupported sailors advanced down the open beach into a deadly hail of rifle fire and canister from Confederates rushing to the parapet. Although many of Lamb's guns had been destroyed or dismounted, he retained enough to punish the brigade. In a series of sprints and halts to seek shelter, the sailors and marines moved in bounds, fewer getting up to go forward each time. Confusion reigned as officers fell and order disintegrated. With no covering naval gunfire, Confederate defenders stood in the open and fired into the mass below. It became a slaughter. A few sailors reached the foot of the Northeast Bastion, only to be cut down from above. Under withering fire and without direction, the sailors and marines broke. The naval brigade quickly degenerated into a disorganized mob fleeing back up the beach. The Confederates cheered and catcalled the fleeing naval force, unaware the fort had been breached elsewhere.

As the sailors and marines began their charge, Terry's lead brigade advanced from its wooded cover. Once in the open, the soldiers came under fire from the battery on the land face and the two field howitzers that covered the access gate. In addition, a Confederate gun moved forward through a sally port a few hundred yards up the land face and opened an enfilading fire. Despite heavy casualties, the brigade pressed on. Reaching the base of the palisade, the attacking soldiers discovered the Confederate defenders could not fire down on them without being exposed. The Federal troops regrouped and charged the enemy parapet, cresting the top more than twenty feet above, and became enmeshed in hand-to-hand combat. On the right, the 117th New York Infantry charged down the road and across the half-destroyed bridge, straight into the two guns at the entrance gate. The guns fired nearly point-blank into the New Yorkers' faces. Those not killed or wounded closed on the battery, where a melee occurred. The initial onslaught, meeting heavy resistance at the gate and on the parapets, stalled. Observing from a vantage point several hundred yards away, Terry ordered the next brigade to press forward. Sheer numbers began to tell. The Confederates at the gate and the overlooking battery finally gave way. At just about the moment the naval brigade broke, Terry's troops secured a foothold at the other end of the land face. Inadvertently, the sailors and marines had distracted the enemy just long enough to ensure Army success.

Wheeling to their left, the Federal troops assaulted the next battery on the land face, while others advanced in parallel on the flat ground inside the fort. Lamb, previously focused on the naval brigade's charge, suddenly observed the breach

Land face of Fort Fisher looking toward the sea
(Library of Congress)

from his vantage point on the Northeast Bastion and shifted what troops he had to reinforce those already in the fight. The parapet restricted the battle to a continuous series of hand-to-hand fights along a narrow frontage, enabling outnumbered Confederates to match the Federals at the point of contact. Confusion reigned in the bloody close-quarters fighting. Attacking regiments, many of their officers killed or wounded, lost cohesion even as the soldiers pressed on. Repositioned to sweep the plain inside the fort, canister fire from cannons on the sea face prevented any Federal advance on the open ground. Momentarily stalemated, the assault soon regained its momentum. Porter's ships resumed firing on the land face, aided by signals and careful observation of regimental colors. The Confederates, outnumbered and assailed by Federal troops and blasted by accurate naval fire, began to lose heart. Yet as darkness fell and exhaustion on both sides set in, the battle abated with the defenders still in control of half the land face.

Terry refused to let up. He ordered his final brigade to move into the fort and to attack as soon as it could be in position. At 2100, the brigade resumed the assault led by the 3d New Hampshire Infantry, accompanied by many of the troops who had fought all day. The Confederates gave way, too weak and demoralized to resist any longer. Clearing the land face and turning south along the interior base of the sea face, the attack killed, captured, or pushed back the remaining defenders. Some fled to Battery Buchanan to the south, seeking evacuation by boat. The 27th U.S. Colored Troops, redeployed from the northern defensive line, now joined the advance. As they closed on Battery Buchanan, the last defenders surrendered. In a tragic postscript, early on 16 January, the fort's main magazine exploded in a roar, probably after entry by torch-wielding soldiers, killing or burying as many as 200 men, both Federal troops and Confederate prisoners. Fort Fisher had fallen.

With the seizure of Fort Fisher, the port of Wilmington was closed. Yet Grant wanted more than to stop blockade runners; he needed the port and city as a base for Sherman's army as it advanced though the Carolinas. Between Hoke's division and the various garrisons of the Cape Fear defenses, more than 7,000 Confederate troops still stood in the way. Terry lacked the strength for the task, his original force of less than 10,000 depleted by the casualties suffered at Fort Fisher. In a testimony to how far the United States Army had come since 1861, Grant ordered the XXIII Corps, veterans of Sherman's Atlanta Campaign and most recently the Battle of Franklin, Tennessee, to travel east from Nashville by train and board transports for movement to North Carolina. He appointed its commander, Maj. Gen. John M. Schofield, to take personal command of operations. Within three weeks, the lead division from the corps arrived at Fort Fisher. On 11 February, Terry, now under Schofield's direction, advanced up the east side of the Cape Fear only to be stopped by Hoke's division, still dug in to the north. Schofield ferried the division of the XXIII Corps to the west side of the river. On 18 February, supported by Navy gunboats moving in parallel, the division enveloped the Confederate stronghold at Fort Anderson, fifteen miles downriver from Wilmington, forcing the defenders to retreat. With the Federals approaching Wilmington from the west and on the river, Bragg ordered Hoke to withdraw to the city's inner defenses. He made one last stand on 20 February to allow Confederate stores to be evacuated or destroyed. The Confederate forces departed two days later, retreating northward toward Goldsboro. The 3d New Hampshire Infantry led the procession into the city, closely followed by a contingent of U.S. Colored Troops.

The capture of Wilmington all but ended Union operations along the Atlantic coast. Charleston surrendered on 18 February as General Sherman's army stormed through South Carolina. Schofield moved inland in pursuit of Bragg's rebels, directing newly arriving units of the XXIII Corps to sail to New Berne, link with Federal forces there, and drive toward Kinston and Goldsboro from the east. At the Battle of Wyse Fork near Kinston on 7–10 March, they clashed with a Confederate force under Bragg composed of local troops and Hoke's division. Although initially successful, Bragg was outnumbered and facing entrapment by Schofield closing from the south. He retreated to join General Joseph E. Johnston's army withdrawing slowly before Sherman. Bloody rearguard battles at Averasboro and Bentonville in March did little to slow Sherman, who continued to pursue the Confederates toward Raleigh and Durham. On 26 April 1865, Johnston formally surrendered to Sherman. With General Lee's Army of Northern Virginia having already surrendered on 9 April, the American Civil War was finally drawing to a close.

Analysis

Nearly every expedition or battle along the Atlantic coast required Army-Navy cooperation to be successful. Port Royal, Hatteras, Roanoke, New Berne, Morris Island, and Wilmington and countless small forays would have been impossible without it. Along the coast and in the North Carolina inland waters, mobility and firepower depended on naval ships, ranging from large warships to small gunboats. General Lee noted in early 1862 that Federal troops moving up the rivers and inlets of South Carolina and Georgia rarely strayed out of range of naval guns. Garrisons posted on the sea islands of South Carolina or in towns bordering the inland sounds relied on naval forces for their supply and often defense. Thus when naval superiority was lost, as when the ironclad *Albemarle* sallied forth, Union troops fell back and abandoned Plymouth. Once the ironclad was sunk several weeks later, it was the Confederates who quickly withdrew in the face of advancing Federal gunboats. Neither the Navy nor the Army could have succeeded without the other.

Yet, despite their interdependence, cooperation between the two services varied widely, often depending on the personalities involved. Friction between Gillmore and Dahlgren at Charleston and Butler and Porter at Fort Fisher poisoned chances for success. In contrast, the close relationship between Burnside and Goldsborough at Roanoke Island and New Berne proved key to the quick victories.

If personalities played a role, so too did competing strategic goals. The Navy's primary focus lay with the blockade; it did not understand the Army's reticence to support it. The Army viewed the coastal war largely as a sideshow that threatened to drain badly needed soldiers from the main theaters of conflict. The U.S. government never overcame this divergence of priorities.

Bickering aside, over the course of four years of war, Federal military operations along the Atlantic coast played a key role in slowly strangling the Confederacy. Between 1862 and 1865, Southern cotton exports fell to just 5 percent of prewar levels. The number of vessels entering Confederate ports steadily decreased as the war went on. The broad strategy first envisioned by Maj. Gen. Winfield Scott and detailed by the Commission of Conference ultimately proved highly effective.

Bit by bit the North closed off rebel commerce while keeping Southern coastal communities in a state of alarm that tied down the Confederacy's own hard-pressed military manpower. Thus, despite their relatively few numbers and often forgotten efforts, the soldiers who served along the Atlantic coast played a crucial part in the outcome of the Civil War.

The Author

R. Scott Moore is the director of the Field Programs and Historical Services Division at the U.S. Army Center of Military History. He previously served in the Office of the Deputy Assistant Secretary of Defense for Partnership Strategy and as a senior defense analyst at Hicks and Associates. A Marine Corps infantry officer from 1976 to 2001, he participated in combat, expeditionary, and humanitarian operations in Panama, the Balkans, Kuwait, the Far East, and Africa and commanded a battalion landing team during noncombatant evacuation operations in Albania in 1997. Moore graduated from the U.S. Naval Academy in 1976, earned a master's degree in history from Duke University, a master's degree in international relations from Salve Regina University, and a Ph.D. in conflict analysis and resolution from George Mason University. He is a graduate of the Marine Corps Command and Staff College.

Further Readings

Browning, Robert M., Jr. *From Cape Charles to Cape Fear: The North Atlantic Blockading Squadron during the Civil War.* Tuscaloosa, Ala.: University of Alabama Press, 1993.

———. *Success Is All That Was Expected: The South Atlantic Blockading Squadron during the Civil War.* Washington, D.C.: Brassey's, 2002.

Dobak, William A. *Freedom by the Sword: The U.S. Colored Troops, 1862–1867.* Washington, D.C.: U.S. Army Center of Military History, 2011.

Fonvielle, Chris E., Jr. *The Wilmington Campaign: Last Rays of Departing Hope.* Campbell, Calif.: Savas Publishing, 1997.

Nulty, William H. *Confederate Florida: The Road to Olustee.* Tuscaloosa, Ala.: University of Alabama Press, 1990.

Trotter, William R. *Ironclads and Columbiads: The Civil War in North Carolina, The Coast.* Winston-Salem, N.C.: John F. Blair, Publisher, 1989.

For more information on the U.S. Army in the Civil War, please read other titles in the U.S. Army Campaigns of the Civil War series published by the U.S. Army Center of Military History (www.history.army.mil).

Made in the USA
Lexington, KY
17 May 2018